GUIDE TO
PERU

MARION MORRISON

Highlights for Children

CONTENTS

On the cover: The ruins of Machu Picchu, the "lost city" of the Inca people, with Mt. Huayna Picchu in the background

NORTH AMERICA

Tropic of Cancer

Equator

Peru   SOUTH AMERICA

Tropic of Capricorn

Published by Highlights for Children
© 1996 Highlights for Children, Inc.
P.O. Box 18201
Columbus, Ohio 43218-0201
1-800-962-3661

10 9 8 7 6 5 4 3
ISBN 0-87534-929-3

EUROPE

ASIA

AFRICA

AUSTRALIA

ANTARCTICA

△ **Peru's flag** The red and white flag dates from 1825. The emblem in the center shows a vicuña and a cinchona tree. In the lower half is a horn of plenty filled with gold coins.

PERU AT A GLANCE

Area 496,225 square miles (1,285,216 square kilometers)

Population 22,125,000

Capital Lima, population 6,484,000

Other big cities Arequipa (population 820,470), Callao (638,200), Trujillo (508,700)

Highest mountain Huascarán, 22,205 feet (6,768 meters)

Longest river Ucayali, 1,700 miles (2,736 kilometers), including Apurimac River

Largest lake Lake Titicaca, part in Peru 1,913 square miles (4,957 square kilometers)—remainder is in Bolivia

Official languages Spanish and Quechua

▽ **Peruvian stamps** The designs below show objects made by the ancient civilizations along the Peru coast, a fire service vehicle, and the Spaniards arriving in Peru by ship.

▷ **Peruvian money** Peru's currency is the *Nuevo Sol*, or New Sol (S). On the S20 note is the Torre Tagle Palace, a fine colonial building in Lima. The S50 note shows a lakeside town in Peru.

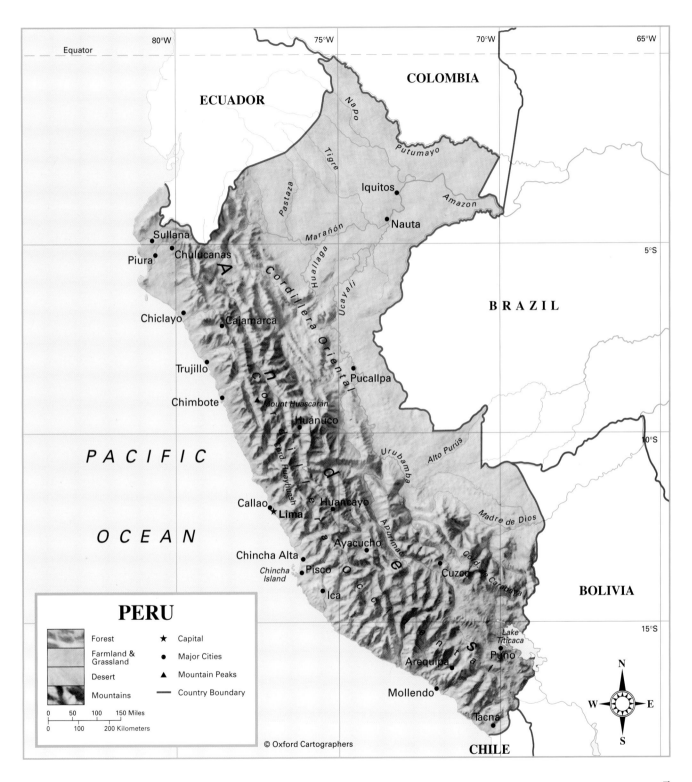

PACIFIC

OCEAN

ECUADOR

COLOMBIA

BRAZIL

BOLIVIA

CHILE

Equator

80°W
75°W
70°W
65°W

5°S

10°S

15°S

Napo

Tigre

Pastaza

Putumayo

Iquitos

Nauta

Amazon

Marañón

Huallaga

Ucayali

Sullana

Piura

Chulucanas

A

Cordillera Oriental

Chiclayo

Cajamarca

c

Trujillo

h

Chimbote

▲ *Mount Huascarán*

Huánuco

Pucallpa

Urubamba

Alto Purús

Card. Huayhuash

d

Callao

★ Lima

Huancayo

Apurímac

e

Madre de Dios

Chincha Alta

Chincha Island

Pisco

Ayacucho

o

c

c

Ica

Cuzco

Cord. de Carabaya

n

t

a

Arequipa

Lake Titicaca

Puno

l

Mollendo

Tacna

PERU

	Forest		★	Capital
	Farmland & Grassland		●	Major Cities
	Desert		▲	Mountain Peaks
	Mountains		—	Country Boundary

0   50   100   150 Miles

0   100   200 Kilometers

© Oxford Cartographers

N

W   E

S

WELCOME TO PERU

Peru lies in the west of South America. It is the continent's third-largest country after Brazil and Argentina. It borders five other countries—Ecuador, Colombia, Brazil, Bolivia, and Chile—and the Pacific Ocean to the west. All of Peru lies within the tropics, but the land and climate vary greatly.

Peru can be split into three regions: the coast, the mountains, and the Amazon River basin. A narrow desert runs all the way along the coast. The desert is crossed by rivers, so there are green oases. Lima, Peru's capital city, is in this region. The massive Andes mountain range fills the center of the country. Many peaks are snow covered all year round, but people live and work in the high valleys. The Amazon rain forests cover almost one-third of the country, but very few people live here. Many large rivers flow eastward from the mountains, winding through the forests for hundreds of miles before joining the mighty Amazon River. The rain forest area is known as the *selva*. At least 80 inches (200 centimeters) of rain fall on the selva each year.

Hundreds of years ago, civilizations grew up in the river valleys of the coast. But by A.D. 1500 the Incas from the highlands had conquered the coastal peoples. The Inca Empire stretched from Ecuador through Peru to Chile, and included parts of Bolivia. The Incas had a powerful army, but their empire was conquered by Spanish invaders early in the 1500s. Years of colonial rule followed. Peru finally became independent from Spain in 1824.

Today the population of Peru is made up mostly of people native to South America, mainly the Quechua, and descendents of mixed marriages between the Quechua and the Spanish settlers. Most Quechua still live in the mountains, their traditional home.

△ **Quechua natives** The styles of their hats can often tell you which village or town they come from. These women are from the highland town of Pisac, near Cuzco.

◁ **The Vilcanota Valley**
Mt. Saguacitay overlooks
the valley and the village
of Taray in the foreground.
Also known as the Sacred
Valley of the Incas, it is near
the city of Cuzco.

△ **The Inca festival of Inti
Raimi, the festival of the
Sun** It is celebrated at the
fortress of Sacsayhuaman,
near Cuzco, on June 24. It is
a big tourist attraction.

7

THE CITY OF KINGS

Lima, the "City of Kings," was founded by the Spanish leader Francisco Pizarro on January 18, 1535. For almost three hundred years Lima was the most important city in Spanish South America. You can still see relics of its colonial history, such as the cathedral and the city's central square, the Plaza de Armas. The Presidential Palace, completed in 1938 on the site of Pizarro's Palace, is also on the Plaza de Armas. If you go down Jirón de la Unión, one of the main shopping streets, you will come to the Plaza San Martín and the newer part of Lima where there are more modern buildings.

From there you can take a bus or taxi to the districts of Lima, or suburbs. Some, like Miraflores, are well known for their wealth and grand buildings. There are also many skyscrapers. These buildings are specially built to resist earthquakes.

◁ **The Plaza San Martín in Lima** In the center is a statue of General José de San Martín. Born in Argentina, he fought to free Argentina, Chile, and Peru from Spanish rule.

▷ **At the Plaza de Acho bullring in Lima** Before a bullfight, the horses, or *Caballos de Paso*, parade in front of the crowd. The Plaza de Acho bullring is the oldest in the Americas.

Some of Lima's other suburbs are poor. Further inland there are large shantytowns, or *Pueblos Jóvenes* (young towns). These have been hastily built by the many hundreds of people who are moving all the time from country areas into the city. Today about half of all Peru's town dwellers live in and around Lima.

For several months of the year Lima is covered by a dull gray mist, or *garúa*, and the weather is damp and cold. The air is very moist. When the sun appears during the summer (November to March), people head for the beaches to enjoy sun, sand, and sea. Some have summer homes there.

Lima has many excellent museums, including a new National Museum and an underground Gold Museum. Here you can see weavings, pottery, and the superb gold craftsmanship of Peru's early civilizations.

△ **The Archbishop's Palace, Lima** The palace stands next to the cathedral on the Plaza de Armas. Its beautiful wooden balconies date from 1924 when the palace was rebuilt.

THE DESERT COAST

The Pan American Highway runs all the way down the west side of South America from Colombia to Chile. The coast is generally a dry area without frequent rain, although heavy rains do fall occasionally. These rains are said to be caused by El Niño, the "Christ Child," because they often occur around Christmas. They are the result of warm waters from near the equator meeting the cold waters of the Humboldt current off the Peru coast.

The road going south from Lima passes through several river valleys. People have lived here for more than a thousand years. One of the best-known areas is the Nazca Valley, famous for the drawings the ancient Nazcas left on the desert plains. The designs show animals and birds, as well as a pattern of straight lines. They are so large that the best way to see them is from an airplane. Another ancient culture from the region, the Paracas, is well known for weaving. Wrappings around mummies have been discovered. Many people think they are some of the finest weavings ever made.

Today people in the valleys farm, as their ancestors did. With irrigation from the rivers, land is fertile. Cotton, sugarcane, vegetables, and fruit are grown. Grapes brought to the Ica Valley by Spaniards are used for wine and the local *pisco* brandy.

Peru's coastal waters are normally rich with fish, such as flounder, sole, and shellfish. The main fish caught is the anchovy. Sometimes, due to overfishing and the effects of El Niño, the fish move southward. When this happens, it is a disaster for thousands of seabirds, such as cormorants, boobies, and pelicans. The best places to see the birds are at the Paracas National Reserve or the Ballestas Islands.

▽ **Sea lions on the Ballestas Islands** The bird droppings, or *guano*, on the rocks have been used as a fertilizer for hundreds of years.

◁ **Designs drawn on the Nazca Desert** Among them are a monkey, spider, whale, and lizard. There are several birds. One is thought to be a condor. This one is known as the Hummingbird.

▽ **Preparing raw cotton for the local mills** Cotton has been grown on the Peruvian coast for a long time. It was used by the early peoples for their weaving.

AMONG THE VOLCANOES

Before you reach the border with Chile, you can follow the Pan American Highway into the city of Arequipa, Peru's second-largest city. It is an uphill climb from sea level to almost 8,000 feet (2,438 meters) and takes about three hours by car. On the way, stop to see the strange crescent-shaped, ash-gray sand dunes about halfway along the route. Arequipa lies in a beautiful valley at the foot of El Misti volcano. This volcano was important to the ancient Inca people. In the same range is Peru's highest volcano, Coropuna, 21,079 feet (6,425 meters) high. Coropuna is an active volcano.

▽ **El Misti** This volcano is 19,102 feet (5,822 meters) high. Cattle graze on the slopes below, and farmers grow crops such as barley, corn, beans, and potatoes.

△ **The main square, the Plaza de Armas, in Arequipa** Some of the buildings on the square were founded in the 1600s.

▷ **The Colca Canyon** The best time to visit the canyon is from April to November. It was discovered in the 1500s by Spanish missionaries.

Earthquakes have destroyed Arequipa more than once. Because of the danger from earthquakes, most buildings have only one story. Many of them are built of sillar, a pearly-white material produced by volcanic eruptions. Sillar is strong, but it can be carved easily. Wonderful carvings decorate the cathedral, many churches, houses, and even movie theaters.

The Santa Catalina Convent is well worth a visit. For years, up to 450 nuns lived here, shut away from the outside world except for women servants. Now it is open for visitors to see the flower-filled cloisters, the white-, brown-, and blue-painted houses, and the maze of cobblestone streets. It is all beautifully kept as a miniature town.

While in Arequipa, spend a day visiting the Colca Canyon and the village of Chivay. The Colca Canyon, said to be twice as deep as the Grand Canyon, is surrounded by a patchwork of terraced fields. The women of Chivay wear particularly lovely costumes.

13

LAKE TITICACA

It is a long day's drive from Arequipa to Lake Titicaca, but the marvelous scenery makes the trip worth it. First try the climb to the highest point at Abra Toroya, almost 15,400 feet (4,694 meters) above sea level. Here you may feel short of breath. Some people do suffer from altitude sickness, or *soroche*, but it is usually not a problem if you move slowly. Along the route watch out for llamas. You may also see a vicuña. This smaller relative of the llama is highly valued for its wool. A few years ago the vicuña was close to extinction, but theirs has been a success story. Today it is not so difficult to see them in the wild.

From Abra Toroya the road descends slowly, leaving behind the mountains. You are now heading toward the high, open plain known as the Altiplano. This region is the home of the Aymara people, known for the bowler hats worn by the women. The Aymara lead a hard, poor life, growing crops and tending llamas and sheep. They live in mud-brick adobe huts scattered across the Altiplano. Families often live and sleep in one room. They cook on an open fire or in an outside clay oven. Here, at around 12,000 feet (3,658 meters) above sea level, the climate is fierce. The sun can be very hot, but at night temperatures drop to well below freezing.

Your journey up the mountains ends at Lake Titicaca. The vast, magnificent lake is surrounded by snow-covered mountains. Lake Titicaca is on the border between Peru and Bolivia. It is the world's highest navigable lake. The main town near the lake is Puno. In the Bay of Puno are floating islands made of totora reed. Aymara families live on the islands, where they also have a school for the children.

▷ **Boats on Lake Titicaca** These boats, called *balsas*, are made from bundles of totora reed. The Aymara use them for fishing and transportation.

▷ **Bowler-hatted Aymara women** On floating islands in Lake Titicaca the women are learning to read and write.

▽ **Colorful wool blankets and tapestries** Tourists like to buy these as souvenirs of Peru.

LAND OF THE INCAS

The train from Puno to Cuzco leaves very early in the morning. On the route there are many stops at stations where local people shout and bargain to sell their goods. Rugs, furs, alpaca ponchos, sweaters, and colorful wool *chullo* caps are popular with tourists. There is time to browse along food stalls stacked with snacks of chicken, corn, and stuffed peppers. Or if you want a drink, try Inca Cola, the local soda pop.

Much of the journey is across the flat, open Altiplano before the train climbs to the colder, drier, and even higher region of the Andes known as the *puna*. The highest point on the line is La Raya. Then the train goes down into the Vilcanota Valley and on to Cuzco, which is about 11,500 feet (3,468 meters) above sea level. It was the capital city of the Inca Empire and is believed to be laid out in the shape of a puma wildcat.

△ **A Quechua woman weaving on a loom**
She will probably use the striped cloth to make a poncho, shawl, or blanket.

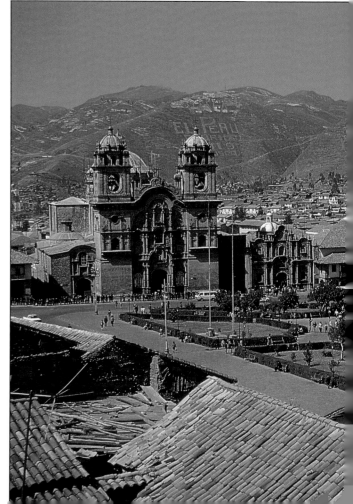

16

The Incas began as a small tribe in the Cuzco Valley around A.D. 1200. They created a vast, strong empire. They had no written language but used a knotted string device called a *quipu* to keep a record of accounts. All people had to work if they could, but the weak and sick were well cared for. There was plenty of food for everyone.

The Incas were good engineers and builders. Roads connected Cuzco to all parts of the empire. They built temples and palaces of huge stone blocks without using mortar. The well-trained army conquered many new lands. But when the Spaniards arrived in 1532, the Inca Empire was in the middle of a civil war. The Inca Emperor Atahualpa, tricked by the Spaniards, was captured and later executed. The Spaniards took Cuzco and, less than 300 years after it began, the Inca Empire collapsed.

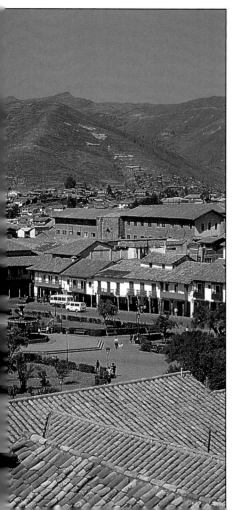

◁ **The Plaza de Armas at the heart of Cuzco** The Jesuit church of La Compañia was built in 1576 where the Inca Palace of the Serpents once stood.

△ **A fine example of Inca building** Sacsayhuaman is a fort overlooking Cuzco. The stone blocks fit so closely that a knife blade will not fit between them.

MACHU PICCHU—A LOST CITY

The most famous of the Inca sites around Cuzco is Machu Picchu. From Cuzco it takes about four hours by tourist train to get there. You may prefer to leave the train at Ollantaytambo and walk along the Inca Road, which leads to Machu Picchu. The hike takes between three and five days, crossing very high passes, but the views make all the effort worthwhile. At night it is very cold, so make sure you have a warm sleeping bag and a tent.

When the Inca Empire collapsed, people escaped from Cuzco. For many years there were rumors of a "lost city" in the jungle. When the American explorer Hiram Bingham found Machu Picchu in 1911, it was covered in forest. The ruins are at the top of a hill, and to reach them you leave the train and take a bus that zigzags its way up the hillside. You will see the stone walls of temples, palaces, and houses, as well as parts of staircases, irrigation canals, and the famous Sun Dial. For the best view, climb up Huayna Picchu, the hill that overlooks the site. But be careful—it is very steep.

Quechua people live in the villages and valleys near Cuzco. Some speak only the Quechua language. They live in adobe mud huts and spend much of the day herding llamas, sheep, and alpacas. They grow corn, potatoes, and quinoa, a protein-rich cereal. Although they lead hard, simple lives, Quechua people dress in some of the most colorful clothing you will see anywhere in Peru. At festival time they dance to music played on panpipes or on the *charango*, which looks like a small guitar. Women wear large hats decorated with fringes and flowers, embroidered jackets, and full skirts. Men wear long, richly colored ponchos.

▷ **The Pisac Sunday market** Traders from Cuzco and the Quechua from their villages come to exchange goods and sell crafts to tourists.

▷ **The village of Chincheros** The modern adobe mud church was built on top of old Inca walls.

△ **Terraces at Machu Picchu** In Inca times, these were irrigated and used for growing corn and other crops. The houses at the end of the terraces have mostly been restored with new thatch.

A Jungle Reserve

To the northeast of Cuzco are the vast Amazon lowland forests that extend into Brazil. To reach them you follow a twisting road that drops steeply down the forested slopes of the east Andes. There are hairpin turns and deep gulleys on either side. At dawn, from a high point called Tres Cruces, you get an amazing view as the sun breaks through the cloud-covered forests far below.

Most visitors join a tour to see the forest. There are several national parks. Manu National Park is the largest. You can travel through the park by canoe or other riverboat, and you can stay in a jungle lodge. In the Manu River and nearby lakes you may see giant otters and caimans. If you are very lucky, you might also see an anaconda, the largest Amazonian snake.

You will need a guide to take you on a hike through the forest, because it is easy to get lost. There are giant trees with buttress roots and lianas hanging from the canopy. In the undergrowth there are many spiders and insects. You will certainly see colorful birds such as toucans, parrots, and macaws. And even if you do not see any monkeys, you may hear the harsh call of the red howler monkeys echoing through the trees.

Large areas of the forest have now been cleared for commercial use, and most of Peru's oil comes from the Amazon lowlands. Few people live here except settlers and small groups of forest Indians. The Indians live by hunting, fishing, and growing a few crops much as they always have done. Their homes are still wood and thatch, and they cook on open fires. But they are meeting more people from the outside world. In some villages there are schools and medical clinics. Many also now have transistor radios and cook with metal pots and pans.

▷ Machiguenga Indians

Three of the men sitting in the boats are wearing the traditional long cotton robes that are called *cushmas*. The Machiguenga trade salt and other goods with settlers.

▽ An Amazonian jaguar

Trade in jaguar skins, for use as rugs and fashionable clothing, is now banned by law in Peru.

▽ **Nahua Indians** Contact was made with the Nahua people for the first time in 1986. This man and his wife are using bird feathers to make a headdress.

MAGNIFICENT MOUNTAINS

Along the coast from Lima northward to Ecuador, much of the land is desert. Where it is crossed by rivers, fertile oasis valleys have grown up. Chimbote is Peru's largest fishing port. A new port has also been built there for the steel industry, and the area is badly polluted.

Ruins of several ancient civilizations have survived along the coast. Among them is the large mud pyramid of the Chimú at Paramonga. South of Chimbote is Sechín, a large square temple dating from about 3,500 years ago. Its walls are covered with dozens of gruesome carvings—heads, legs, and arms cut off in battle.

Just south of Paramonga a road leads into the mountains and to the Callejón de Huaylas. For many people this is the most spectacular part of Peru. It is a region of snow-covered mountains, deep gorges, glaciers, turquoise-colored glacier lakes, streams filled with trout, masses of flowers, and many hummingbirds. It was also the scene of Peru's worst natural disaster. More than 60,000 people were killed in an earthquake and the landslide that followed it in 1970. Towns such as Caraz and Yungay were almost completely destroyed. Today they have mostly been restored.

Huaraz is the capital of the region, and from the town there are magnificent views of the snowy peaks of the Cordillera Blanca. Huascarán, Peru's highest mountain, is one of the peaks you can see. Huaraz is also the main center for the hikers and mountain climbers who now come from all over the world to climb and walk in the Callejón de Huaylas. Huaraz is also the best base for a trip to see the ruins of Chavín de Huantar where you will find some of the finest stone carvings in all of South America.

▷ **In Miraflores, one of Lima's largest and most prosperous suburbs** Miraflores is a seaside suburb and has many excellent hotels, restaurants, shops, fine houses, and parks.

▽ **The alpaca, a relative of the llama** It looks similar but is smaller. Alpacas are world famous for their wool, which is used to make sweaters and ponchos.

▽ **Harvesting sugarcane on a coastal plantation** Almost half of Peru's population lives within the narrow coastal strip of the country.

THE FAR NORTH

North of Chimbote are three major towns, Trujillo, Chiclayo, and Piura, founded by the Spaniards in the 1500s. Trujillo competes with Arequipa to be Peru's second city. Near Trujillo is Chan Chan, the famous ruins of the Chimú people. Chan Chan was the world's largest adobe-mud city. Within its walls are ruins of palaces, temples, streets, and houses, some with molded decorations. The Chimú were the last of the coastal cultures to fall to the Incas, in A.D. 1450.

Also close to Trujillo are the enormous pyramids of the Moche culture, the Huaca del Sol and the Huaca de la Luna, shrines to the Sun and Moon. The Moche were skilled craftsmen, but they are also known for their engineering works. They built canals and irrigated the land. The agricultural state of Lambayeque, with Chiclayo as its capital, owes much to this ancient people.

The city of Cajamarca lies in the Andes Mountains to the northeast of Trujillo. An attractive colonial town, it is famous as the place where Francisco Pizarro imprisoned the Inca Emperor Atahualpa. Pizarro had promised to release Atahualpa once a room had been filled with gold, but he did not keep his promise.

Separating Chiclayo from the city of Piura is the Sechura Desert. A large area of shifting sands, the Sechura is irrigated by local rivers and by water brought from the Amazon to the Pacific coast through a tunnel in the Andes. Cotton is grown here. Further north are the Talara oilfields.

Along the northern Pacific coast you can see rafts of balsa wood similar to those used by the Incas. They were copied by Thor Heyerdahl for his Kon-Tiki raft, which he sailed from Peru across the Pacific in 1947.

◁ **Boats made of totora reed** Similar to the balsas on Lake Titicaca, they are known on the coast as *caballitos*, or "little horses."

▷ **El Señor de Sipan** Gold masks like this one of a Moche priest were among precious objects found in the royal tombs of Sipan in northern Peru. The Moche people were master craftsmen in gold.

▽ **Burial figures high on a cliffside at Carajia** Chachapoyas was the home of the Chachas before they were driven out by the Incas between 1450 and 1470.

OVER THE TOP TO THE AMAZON

The Central Railroad of Peru runs from Lima to the Andean town of Huancayo. It is the world's highest train line and the journey is spectacular. The line climbs from sea level to its highest point at 15,690 feet (4,782 meters) in 99 miles (159 kilometers). It does not always carry passengers.

If you cannot take the train, take the Central Highway to La Oroya. Here you begin an exciting road journey down to the Amazon lowlands. You descend quickly from the bleak mountain ranges to dense green forest, following the tumbling Huallaga River. First stop is the town of Tingo Maria, a center for growing coca. Coca leaves are used to make a drink that is like tea.

From Tingo Maria to Pucallpa, where the road stops, you follow a magnificent pass through forested mountains. The cliffs on either side are 2,000 feet (610 meters) high. Then the road goes through a canyon with walls covered in ferns, strange flowers called bromeliads, leafy plants, and small waterfalls. The last part of the journey across the lowlands is now mostly cleared land, where cattle graze and crops grow.

▷ **Steam train on the Central Railroad** A steam train still runs on the narrow gauge line from Huancayo to the mining town of Huancavelica.

The jungle town of Pucallpa is on the Ucayali River, which flows into the Amazon River. It is the last port that Amazon boats can reach. Getting from Pucallpa to Iquitos, the main city in the Amazon part of Peru, takes six days by river—there is no road!

In the late 1800s, Iquitos benefited from a rubber boom, and in the 1900s from the oil and timber industries. The city has some historic buildings and a population of over 285,000. From Iquitos you can take a direct flight back to Lima—a trip of less than two hours—to end your journey.

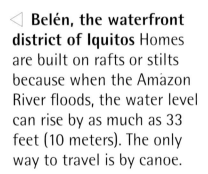

◁ **Belén, the waterfront district of Iquitos** Homes are built on rafts or stilts because when the Amazon River floods, the water level can rise by as much as 33 feet (10 meters). The only way to travel is by canoe.

▷ **An Amazon riverboat carrying tourists** Boats like this once carried rubber, which was discovered in the Amazon in the late 1800s. It brought great wealth to Iquitos and other Amazon towns.

PERU FACTS AND FIGURES

People

Most Peruvians are *mestizos*, or descendents of mixed marriages between the native peoples and the Spanish settlers.

The native highland American peoples are the Quechua and Aymara. They are sometimes called *campesino,* a word that means "of the countryside" and refers to Indians and other people who live in rural areas. Amazonian Indian groups include the Machiguenga, the Campa, and the Shipibo.

Immigrant nationalities include the Chinese, brought in to work on the railways, Africans to work on sugar plantations, and the Japanese, who are now the largest ethnic minority.

Trade and Industry

Mining has always been an important part of the Peruvian economy. Copper and iron deposits are found on the southern coast, while silver, gold, lead, and zinc are found in the highlands.

Most of Peru's oil comes from the northeast Amazon region, but there are also oilfields in the

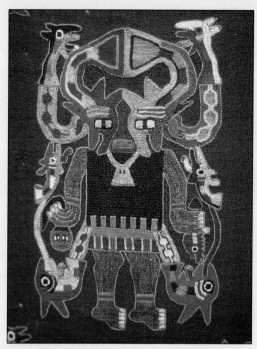

△ **Ancient design** It is about 2000 years old and comes from a cloth found in a mummy bundle in a grave at Paracas on the Peru coast.

north, near the coast. Production is enough to supply about half of the energy that the country needs. Energy is also supplied by hydro-electric plants built on some of Peru's many rivers. Wood is also used as fuel and to supply paper mills and plywood factories.

About 10 percent of workers are employed in manufacturing industries, most of which are in or close to Lima. The factories produce processed foods, textiles, footwear, cars and other vehicles, paper, chemicals, and plastics.

Fishing

Peru has traditionally been a leading producer of fishmeal that is used for fertilizer and animal feed. It is now second-biggest in the world. At certain times of the year, Peru prohibits fishing of some species, such as young anchovies and sardines, to help protect the species.

Farming

About one-third of Peru's population is involved in farming. This includes small farmers in the highlands as well as large-scale farming on the coast. In the oasis valleys cotton, sugar, rice, and fruit are important crops. Coffee is the main export crop. New crops that have been introduced include strawberries and asparagus. In the south of the country, sheep, poultry, and cattle are raised.

Peru still buys wheat, edible oils, and dairy products from abroad. The government would like to see the small highland farmers produce more of the food they need, as was done in Inca times. But farming in the highlands is hard. The soil is poor and the climate is harsh.

Food

On the coast the most popular food is fish. Dishes include *ceviche* (raw fish, onions, and red peppers marinated in lime juice), *escabeche* (fish with onions, peppers, eggs, olives, and cheese), and *chupe de camarones* (shrimp stew). Favorite meat dishes are *ollucos con charqui* (tuber, a type of potato, with dried meat), *anticuchos* (beef hearts, marinated in vinegar, garlic, and peppers, grilled and served on a skewer), *papa a la Huancaína* (potato with spicy cheese sauce), and *lomo saltado* (a spicy beef stew). Soups are often a meal on their own. For a snack try *empanadas* (pastry sandwiches filled with meat or chicken).

To drink, in addition to coffee and tea, there is *pisco*, a local brandy, *chicha de jora*, a maize beer, or *chicha morada*, a soft drink made with purple maize.

Schools

By law children aged six to fifteen must attend school. But some do not, especially among the poor families of the highlands where the nearest school may be miles away.

△ **The festival of Corpus Christi in Cuzco**
This statue of the Virgin of Almudena is one of many paraded during this important celebration.

Education is free, and schools are run by the State and the Catholic Church. Often in the towns, where there are not enough classrooms, two sessions of lessons are taught each day. The young children go in the morning, and the older in the afternoon.

Higher education is provided by universities and technical institutes. The University of San Marcos in Lima is one of the oldest in the Americas. About ninety percent of Peruvians can read and write fluently.

The Media

Most regions of Peru have daily newspapers, but the best known are produced in Lima. *El Comercio*, *Ojo*, and *Expreso* are the most popular. There is also an English-language magazine, *The Lima Times*. Magazines from the U.S. and Europe are sold, covering topics from hobbies to politics.

There are over 500 radio stations reaching all parts of the country, and the radio is also used for education. Lima has eight television stations. All channels are in Spanish.

Art

The weavings, goldwork, pottery, and stone-block constructions of the ancient Peruvians are some of the oldest, finest and most well-known artifacts ever created.

During the colonial Spanish period, some grand cathedrals, churches, and houses were built.

Weaving is still a traditional craft among the Quechua and Aymara, and pottery is still made.

Among the best-known artists today are the sculptor Joaquín Roca Rey and the painters José Sabogal and Fernando de Szyszlo.

Peru Facts and Figures

Music

The music of the Peruvian highlands is a mixture of Spanish and Andean traditions. The most popular form of dance in the highlands is the *wayno*. The music of the coast has Spanish and African roots, and the best-known dance is the rhythmic *marinera*.

The Spaniards introduced stringed instruments such as the harp and the violin as well as the guitar, which the Peruvians adapted into the small *charango*. Andean instruments range from the panpipes, or *sicu,* to the *quena,* a form of flute. These instruments are often backed by drums, especially at fiesta time.

Religion

Most Peruvians are officially Roman Catholics, the religion introduced by the Spaniards. But in practice many, especially in rural areas, still revere their own gods and spirits, such as Pachamama, goddess of the earth. Some important Catholic and Inca festivals now occur at much the same time, such as Corpus Christi and The Inca Festival of the Sun; both take place in June in Cuzco.

△ **A Quechua man herds his llamas** Across the high plains in Peru's Andean region, llamas are used as pack animals.

Festivals and Holidays

Many national holidays in Peru are based on the religious calendar.
January 1 **New Year's Day**
May 1 **Labor Day**
June 24 **Day of the Peasant**
June 29 **St. Peter's and St. Paul's Day**
July 28 & 29 **Independence Days**
August 30 **St. Rose of Lima** (Patron saint of Peru)
October 8 **Battle of Angamos**
October 18-28 **Lord of the Miracles**
November 1 **All Saints Day**
December 8 **Immaculate Conception**
December 25 **Christmas Day**
Other familiar religious holidays include **Maundy Thursday**, **Good Friday**, and **Easter**.

Plants

Trees include valuable hardwoods, species that produce latex, and palms with nuts, tough fibers, and fruits. In the mountain rain forest there are colorful flowers, such as orchids. Fruits include papaya, custard-apple, passionfruit, guava, and mango.

Animals

The animals most often associated with Peru are the llama and the related alpaca, vicuña, and guanaco. The best known of many birds is the Andean Condor. In the rain forests there are many different species, ranging from the jaguar and ocelot to the tapir and the capybara. There are monkeys, opossums, armadillos, porcupines, sloths, and anteaters, as well as caiman and snakes, vast numbers of insects, fish, and spiders.

Sports

Soccer, or *futbol*, is Peru's national sport, but basketball, volleyball, and gymnastics are also popular. Spectator sports include horseracing and bullfighting. Only the wealthy play golf and tennis, but many people take part in watersports.

HISTORY

People first lived in Peru 20,000 years ago. From about 1200 B.C., cultures such as Chavín in the highlands and Sechín on the coast began to develop. The Paracas-Nazca civilizations flourished from about 700 B.C. to A.D. 500 and the Moche-Chimú from 200 B.C. to A.D. 1400. The Incas emerged about A.D. 1200 and created an immense empire.

The Incas fell to the Spaniards, led by Francisco Pizarro, in 1532. Colonial Peru lasted under the Spaniards until independence was declared on July 28, 1821, by the Argentinian hero José de San Martín. Independence was secured by Símon Bolívar, who had helped to free Venezuela, Colombia, and Ecuador. Bolívar defeated the Spaniards at the Battle of Ayacucho in 1824.

During the rest of the 1800s, Peru was ruled well by Ramón Castilla but went to war with Spain over the rich guano islands off the coast. Peru also joined Bolivia in a war with Chile over nitrate deposits in the Atacama Desert. Peru and Bolivia lost territory as well as the nitrate.

Peru has recently had both military and civilian governments. Some have tried to improve social conditions and introduce land reform. Twice-president Fernando Belaunde Terry had ambitious plans to open up the Amazon. But from 1980, the Sendero Luminoso (Shining Path) terrorist group disrupted the country. In 1990 Alberto Fujimori became the first president of Peru of Japanese descent. He had the terrorist leader arrested, and conditions have improved.

LANGUAGE

Spanish is an official language of Peru, and most people speak or understand it. Quechua became an official language in 1975. In some remote areas, natives speak only Quechua. The Aymara living in the south of the country also have their own language. Indians in the lowland Amazon forests have their own native languages and few know any Spanish. In fact there are more than sixty tribal languages. Many Peruvians speak English, French, or German, which are taught in schools and colleges.

Useful words and phrases

English	Spanish
One	Uno
Two	Dos
Three	Tres
Four	Cuatro
Five	Cinco
Six	Seis
Seven	Siete
Eight	Ocho
Nine	Nueve
Ten	Diez
Sunday	Domingo
Monday	Lunes
Tuesday	Martes
Wednesday	Miércoles

Useful words and phrases

English	Spanish
Thursday	Jueves
Friday	Viernes
Saturday	Sábado
Good morning	Buenos días
Good afternoon	Buenas tardes
Good night	Buenas noches
Good-bye	Adiós
Please	Por favor
Thank you	Gracias
Yes	Sí
No	No
Can you speak English?	¿Habla usted Inglés?
Excuse me	Perdóneme

INDEX

Acknowledgments
Book created for Highlights for Children, Inc. by Bender Richardson White.
Editors: Peter MacDonald and Lionel Bender
Designer: Malcolm Smythe
Art Editor: Ben White
Editorial Assistant: Madeleine Samuel
Picture Researcher: Lionel Bender
Production: Kim Richardson

Maps produced by Oxford Cartographers, England.
Banknotes from Thomas Cook Currency Services.
Stamps from Stanley Gibbons.

Editorial Consultant: Andrew Gutelle
Guide to Peru is approved by the Embassy of Peru, London
Peru Consultant: Lilly C. de Cueto, Lima, Peru
Managing Editor, Highlights New Products: Margie Hayes Richmond

Picture credits
SAP = South American Pictures/Tony Morrison.
t = top, b = bottom, r = right, l= left, c = center.
Cover: SAP/Tony Morrison.
Pages: 6a: SAP. 7a: SAP. 7b: SAP. 8a: SAP. 9a: SAP. 9b: SAP. 10a Kim Richardson/Alba Publishing. 11a: SAP. 11b: SAP. 12a SAP 13a SAP 13b SAP . 14a: SAP. 15a: SAP. 15b: SAP. 16a: SAP. 16b: SAP. 17a: Kim Richardson/Alba Publishing. 18a: SAP. 19a: SAP. 19b: SAP. 20a: SAP. 21a: SAP. 21b: SAP. 22a: SAP 22b: SAP 22c: SAP. 24a: SAP. 25a: SAP. 25b: SAP. 26a: SAP. 27a: SAP. 27b: SAP. 28: SAP. 29: SAP. 30: SAP.
Illustration on page 1 by Tom Powers.